Driving the Scenic Route

Barns of Michigan

By

Robert Aldrich

Copyright © 2023 by – Robert Aldrich – All Rights Reserved.

It is not legal to reproduce, duplicate, or transmit any part of this document in either electronic means or printed format. Recording of this publication is strictly prohibited.

Dedication

This book is dedicated to those that choose to drive the back roads instead of the freeways, that prefer to smell the clean air of the countryside instead of the smog-filled city air. There's merit to slowing down and enjoying the beauty of Michigan's farms.

Acknowledgement

I'd like to acknowledge the hard work and dedication of my editors at Amazon Publishing. Without them this book would not be finished.

About the Author

After spending over 20 years in Southern California and photographing food for over 350 restaurants, Robert and his wife moved back to their home state of Michigan and settled in Mt Pleasant. Soon, Robert became enamoured with the beauty and unique architecture of Michigan's barns, traveling hundreds of miles on the back roads to capture images of different barns.

Foreword

The history of barns in Michigan is a long and storied one. The first barns in the state were built by Native Americans, who used them to store food and shelter their livestock. When European settlers arrived in the 18th century, they brought with them their own barn-building traditions. These traditions were adapted to the local climate and materials, and over time, a unique style of Michigan barn emerged.

Michigan barns are typically made of wood, and they are often large and sturdy. They are typically divided into two main sections: a hayloft for storing hay and straw, and a lower level for housing livestock. Michigan barns are often decorated with brightly colored paint or with carvings, and they can be found all over the state.

Barns played an important role in the development of Michigan agriculture. They provided a place to store food and shelter livestock, and they were also used for a variety of other purposes, such as threshing grain and making cheese. Barns were also a source of pride for farmers, and they were often built to be large and impressive.

In the 20th century, the number of farms in Michigan began to decline, and as a result, the number of barns also declined. However, there are still many beautiful and historic barns in Michigan, and they are a reminder of the state's agricultural heritage.

Here are some of the different types of barns found in Michigan:

- Gable-roofed barns: These barns have a gable roof, which is a roof that slopes down on two sides from a ridge at the top. Gable-roofed barns were the most common type of barn in Michigan in the 19th century.
- Gambrel-roofed barns: These barns have a gambrel roof, which is a roof that slopes down at a steeper angle on the sides than it does on the ends. Gambrel-roofed barns were popular in Michigan during the late 19th and early 20th centuries.
- Bank barns: These barns are built into a hillside, with the lower level of the barn below ground level. Bank barns were common in Michigan during the 19th century.
- Pole barns: These barns are made of wood poles that are driven into the ground and then covered with a roof. Pole barns are a relatively recent type of barn, and they are becoming increasingly popular in Michigan.

Michigan barns are an important part of the state's history and heritage. They are a reminder of the state's agricultural past, and they are also a beautiful and iconic part of the Michigan landscape.

When I wasn't pitching hay, hauling corn or running a tractor, I was heaving a baseball into his mitt behind the barn.

Bob Feller

The farmer is the only man in our economy who buys everything at retail, sells everything at wholesale, and pays the freight both ways.

John F. Kennedy

At my elementary school, there was a barn outside that they used to say was a Bonnie and Clyde hangout.

Lane Garrison

Another night, I dreamed I saw my father sweeping out the barn floor clean and would not suffer the wheat to be brought in the barn. He appeared to me to be in anger.

Joanna Southcott

Mommy smoked but she didn't want us to. She saw smoke coming out of the barn one time, so we got whipped.

Loretta Lynn

Painted oxide red, tall against the expansive fields of summer crops or winter snow, silhouetted against colored skies of a setting sun, the barns were a dramatic, strong architectural presence, primordial in intent yet graceful in presentation.

Hemalata Dandekar

I used to see movies where they'd put on a play in a barn, but I've never played one.

Ken Berry

This mug of mine is as plain as a barn door. Why should people pay 35 cents to look at it?

Spencer Tracy

I'm at the barn six days a week.

Noah Cyrus

My dream is to have a creativity barn, in my backyard, which is full of musical instruments and every kind of paint and oils and paper, and you can just go in and make something.

Allison Janney

I might get to the barn later, but stay longer, and that's what counts.

Bob Baffert

If a farmer fills his barn with grain, he gets mice. If he leaves it empty, he gets actors.

Walter Scott

Even the southeast side of Grand Rapids must bow to the beauty of a Michigan fall.

Daniel Abbott

Having been let out of the barn once, I know I wouldn't be happy if I were home all the time.

Meryl Streep

You need to have a home to go back to, whether it's a hotel room or a barn. It's only home when he's there.

Genevieve Gorger

Minnesota, where everything seemed rustic and weathered and made to age gracefully.

Richard Dean Anderson

I love Massachusetts for a number of reasons. I once loved a magical girl who lived in a magnificently converted barn, a half-hour or so from Boston. I love winters. I love the snow.

J. D. Souther

We don't see a lot of models for male social interaction. There's sports and barn raisings.

Chuck Palahniuk

I'm just disappointed the folks never took a picture of me when I was five years old jumping off the barn into a haystack with my Superman cape.

Wally Funk

We rip through summer, burning the hours and tearing up the land. Then snow comes like a bandage, and winter heals the wounds.

Jerry Daniels

Me and my cousin started doing CrossFit in my barn, I haven't looked back since.

<u>Rich Froning Jr.</u>

In my barn, everyone gets a fair and equal shot.

Bob Baffert

After clearing the land, planting the orchard, building the house and barn, and surviving the Great Depression, our father died suddenly one winter night when we were small, leaving us to learn about loss before we even knew its name.

Virginia Euwer Wolff

I know that organic farms can be industrial and just as large and impersonal as conventional farms. Sometimes the free-range chickens aren't even allowed outside, and so they cluck-walk, packed tight in a dim lit barn. But organic farms use fewer chemicals.

Lisa Brennan-Jobs

A little and a little, collected together, becomes a great deal; the heap in the barn consists of single grains, and drop and drop make the inundation.

Saadi

In Scotland, I have a huge barn full of woodworking tools. I love working with my hands. I basically just make myself bleed a lot. I'm very accident prone.

Greg Wise

I love being outdoors and being with animals, and when you're on a horse, you have to leave your anxieties and worries behind in the barn. It's very therapeutic.

Deborah Harkness

My favourite thing is to do crossword puzzles. I do the 'New York Times' one every morning. Then I go to the barn to see my horse.

Amber Heard

After a while, you know that the best thing you can do is walk out of the barn.

Wendell Berry

I was supposed to be cleaning out the barn, but I was usually reading romance novels. That's how you grow up to be a triller writer.

Chevy Stevens

When I was so fatigued that I couldn't move, the excitement of going to the barn and getting my foot in the stirrup would make me crawl out of bed.

Ann Romney

I've been taking batting practice in my barn where nobody can see me, so I may be better than anyone thinks.

Garth Brooks

Just to go out to a barn, it's fun. It's kind of like a get-away from the city. And also, I love animals.

<u>Stefanie Scott</u>

Cars let us out of the barn and, while they were at it, destroyed the American nuclear family. As anyone who has had an American nuclear family can tell you, this was a relief to all concerned.

P. J. O'Rourke

'Do you want to take riding lessons?' I thought, 'Oh, gross, dirty.' She was like, 'Okay.' And then I did, and now I'm the one cleaning those damn stalls out. You can't get me away from the barn now.

Kaley Cuoco

Opting out of paying someone to allow animals to die in a barn fire or at the slaughterhouse seems pretty reasonable.

Ingrid Newkirk

It seems that the lies in our culture are about as thick as mosquitoes in northern Michigan in the middle of June.

Unknown

Farming isn't something that can be taught. Each plant tells its own story that has to be read repeatedly.

Kelsey Timmerman

I had forgotten how rich and beautiful is the countryside - the deep topsoil, the wealth of great trees, the lake country of Michigan handsome as a well-made woman, and dressed and jewelled.

John Steinbeck

They were kept warm by herding in all the cattle, keeping them together in a closed space and utilizing their body heat. When it came to barns in the winter BTUs stood for Bunched Together Until Summer.

Joanne Fluke

Do not let a flattering woman coax and wheedle you and deceive you; she is after your barn.

Hesoid

That's Branton, Michigan, by the way. Don't try to find it on a map - you'd need a microscope. It's one of a dozen dinky towns north of Lansing, one of the few that doesn't sound like it was named by a French explorer.

Ernest Hemingway

The God-fearing, churchgoing farmers are all gone. Now they all have TVs on their roofs and orgies in their barns.

Rawl Hage

Round barns are a unique and fascinating part of Michigan's agricultural heritage. They are a testament to the ingenuity and creativity of our state's farmers.

Unknown

Everything in summer Michigan seemed to have a soft shimmer to it, as though God had hung gauze over the sky and softly scattered glitter on all His creations.

Viola Shipman

Earth is here so kind, that just tickle her with a hoe, and she laughs with a harvest.

Douglas Jerrold

Any jackass can kick down a barn, but it takes a good carpenter to build one.

Sam Rayburn

New York had its own otherworldly beauty, stunning in its own sensory-overload sort of way, but a jarring juxtaposition to where Sam had grown up, on a family orchard in northern Michigan.

Viola Shipman

If someone as blessed as I am is not willing to clean out the barn, who will?

Ross Perot

As I look at the barn in my ninth decade, I see the no-smoking sign, rusted and tilting on the unpainted gray clapboard. My grandfather, born in 1875, milked his cattle there a century ago.

Donald Hall

It helps that in Michigan everyone goes inside from November through April. But from May until October, they are outside, on display, and all of a sudden if you are single, you have a window to heaven and no way at all to get in.

Charles Baxter

And I was Dorothy in 'The Wizard of Oz' in a production in my dad's barn.

Jonathan Groff

If I had to describe the scent of Michigan in spring and summer, it wouldn't be a particular smell - blooming wildflowers or boat exhaust off the lake - it would be a color: Green.

Viola Shipman

I want people to be excited about cooling towers and megasheds; they're as much part of our history as the rural barn.

Antony Gormley

It was the smell of Michigan when I was a boy and I wished I could have had a sweet-grass basket to keep it in when we travelled and to have under the mosquito net in the bed at night.

Ernest Hemingway

"It's just that I love my state so much I go to Michigan to steal", he explained with an expression almost beatific.

Nelson Algen

I was so naive I used to sneak out to the back of the barn and do nothing.

Johnnie Carson

Agriculture is the most healthful, most useful and most noble employment of man.

George Washington

Farming looks mighty easy when your plow is a pencil and you're a thousand miles from the corn field.

Dwight D. Eisenhower

It is only the farmer who faithfully plants seeds in the Spring, who reaps a harvest in the Autumn.

B. C. Forbes

When tillage begins, other arts follow. The farmers, therefore, are the founders of human civilization.

Daniel Webster

Agriculture is our wisest pursuit, because it will in the end contribute most to real wealth, good morals & happiness.

Thomas Jefferson

The farmer has to be an optimist, or he wouldn't still be a farmer.

Will Rogers

A good farmer is nothing more nor less than a handy man with a sense of humus.

E. B. White

The ultimate goal of farming is not the growing of crops, but the cultivation and perfection of human beings.

Masanobu Fukuoka

We have neglected the truth that a good farmer is a craftsman of the highest order, a kind of artist.

Wendell Berry

Those too lazy to plow in the right season will have no food at the harvest.

Proverbs 20:4

Even if a farmer intends to loaf, he gets up in time to get an early start.

Edgar Watson Howe